Delphinium Gospel

Poems

Denzel Xavier Scott

ELJ Editions, Ltd. is committed to publishing works of quality and integrity. In that spirit, we are proud to offer this poetry collection to our readers. Names, characters, places, and incidents either are the product of the author's imagination or are used fictitiously, and any resemblance to actual persons, living or dead, business establishments, events, or locales is entirely coincidental.

ISBN: 978-1-942004-68-4

Library of Congress Control Number: 2024936988

Cover Artist: Sonja Dimovska "Heart of Poppies"
Cover Design by ELJ Editions, Ltd.

ELJ Publications (Imprint)
ELJ Editions, Ltd.
P.O. Box 815
Washingtonville, NY 10992

www.elj-editions.com

Praise for *Delphinium Gospel*

"Grief is often the wheelhouse of modern Black Poetry, exposing, reflecting, and making fractals of our spirits and of our survival. In Denzel Scott's *Delphinium Gospel*, we are made to Say the Name of the American-sponsored pains that plague us. The plant, Delphinium, symbolically represents happiness or goodwill, but such are often hard to come by in our most undervalued communities—as over-reported (and often overly exaggerated) as its dangers are. But Scott's *Delphinium Gospel* is a vigilant witness to our everyday joys and to the random and sometimes predictable states of violence systematically designed to contain us. some. Yes. of us. In this new collection, Denzel Scott calls us all to mourn, to recall and bear witness, and to finally acknowledge the only generational wealth most of us will ever know—the communions of Black Life & Spirit. *Delphinium Gospel* stands as a testament to the fact that within our seasons of blood loss, there always has been, *and always will be:* Bloom."

–upfromsumdirst aka Ronald Davis is the author of three poetry collections, *To Emit Teal, Deifying a Total Darkness,* and *The Second Stop is Jupiter.*

"Denzel Xavier Scott uses evocative and sharp language in these poems. He has a beautiful way with language and a compelling story to tell. Each of these pieces feels like a fluid painting to step into, each page a beating heart to behold."

–M.M. Carrigan, Editor-In-Chief of *Taco Bell Quarterly*

"Denzel Scott's *Delphinium Gospel* is a stunning debut from an equally stunning poet. The Cave Canem Prize finalist's debut poetry collection has finally arrived, and a gospel it certainly is. Scott's poems leave it all on the page, a wordsmith bringing truth to power within grief and joy into a way that invites, not intrudes upon the reader to revel in his life. This is a collection I will return to time and time again. I cannot wait to see what he does next."

–Chris L. Butler, Editor-In-Chief of *The Poetry Question*

"Denzel Scott's *Delphinium Gospel* reminds me of the joy to be had when we give ourselves permission to linger. These poems are intent on telling the full story, relishing the details, stretching the rich and complicated syntax of their lines like cotton candy. And when dealing with violence, loss, and grief, Scott also makes a statement about healing, how perhaps lingering and taking up space is a distinct coping mechanism, a way to erode the jagged edges of grief. This collection demonstrates how excess can be a route to precision, to portraying our world and experiences more accurately through the accumulation of language, imagery, and surprise."

–Taylor Byas, author of *I Done Clicked My Heels Three Times*

"*Delphinium Gospel* is a catalogue of grief, selfhood, violence, and reckoning. Throughout the collection, we witness the horrors death plagues the body and the mind. The death of family. The death of a perceived self. The death of faith in systems. We journey in the realms of each, desiring a better outcome for the selves that inhabit these pages. And still, there is something like hope in the midst of the darkness; a small light; a yearning spirit that bleeds through it all: "How alive I am, finally, as a falling legend with the dead.""

–Luther Hughes, author of *A Shiver in the Leaves*

"Go with the flesh and become like delphinium." Denzel Xavier Scott's debut summons into being the "herculean task" of exhuming loss to reincarnate life. Scott navigates memory as a journey of survival to dismantle the brutal monuments of empire and reimagine possibility. These honest-as-flesh, direct, and fiercely vulnerable poems confront all the stakes. From the "burden of salvation" emerges a diaspora of hope: "How alive I am." Scott's poetry is an action of liberation. *Delphinium Gospel* is here to give life."

–Tara Skurtu, author of *The Amoeba Game*

Table of Contents

Moonset: Resurrecting Social Worlds

Acknowledgments

Before I can acknowledge anyone or anything else, I would like to acknowledge God and my family, without whom this collection wouldn't exist. Next, I would like to acknowledge three fellow writers who provided the feedback to get this project to this stage, Zefyr Lisowski, Chris L. Butler, and Luther Hughes, all of whom you should follow on Instagram: @zefrrrrrrrrrrrrrrrrrrrrrrrrrrrr, and Twitter: @clbpoetry, and @lutherxhughes. Love y'all so much, you don't even know.

Moonrise: Womb of Culture

Burying Blackberry with Nightshade

My older brother, Randolph, midnight prince,
black, haloed sun of my mother's world,
was newly twenty-eight years old
when he was sprayed with hateful bullets,
unarmed, in diametric opposition
to the loving-kindness of raindrops.
They ripped through him
in the city of our birth,
Savannah, Georgia,
of looming oaks, silvery moss,
good ol' Southern hospitality and headstones,
in its first, not its only,
mass shooting of 2015.

His girlfriend's ex-boyfriend/
possible former side-piece/
other potential father
of her now seven-year-old
unclaimed daughter,
shot him along with that girlfriend
who was shot twice in the face,
her cousin, who was shot in the hip,
and that cousin's two children who were both shot,
the youngest, the then two-year-old
baby girl, brutally shot in the chest.
Bullets tore through my brother
in the last hours of the first day of that year
and by the dawn of its second,
he, our Helios of Wonder, was the only one dead.

He bled out, a freshly slaughtered hog
on the dirty, hunter-green
carpet of his girlfriend's apartment
in a complex as ferocious
as a hornet's nest
licked by an ol' gray
Savannah slave brick.

When he died, our mother,
cloaked in an obsidian hijab,
our Black Madonna alive again,
followed the burial practice
of their Islamic faith and washed his
corpse, soft and sweet, soft and sweet
making him her newborn once more.

All that did my family suffer,
and yet not even five months
later, my father died from the
grief of burying his firstborn,
his namesake, in the rich uncaring soil.

Now they rest side by side,
behind a plantation,
in the hidden city of Shad,
crowded by our ancestors,
slaves and freemen alike.
So bitter was our tragedy,
so exquisite our rage,
that even biblical vengeance
could not quell our indignation.

Retribution was our birthright
more than a hundred times
and we knew it.
But the gun, the smoking barrel,
hard and hot, new moon black like our love
and its iniquities and creations,

black, blue
black, purpled
deep, like our
royal melanin,

could not be our inheritance
if we wished to remain human
and bury the Phoenix born
in the deaths of our dark beloveds,
sweet blackberry and sweeter nightshade.

Carrying Coffins

In America, it's sad, but practical
to plan for a Black child's funeral—
preacher,
choir,
venue,
coffin,
R.I.P. shirts,
moon white peace lilies,
photo collages,
limousine seating,
repass menu—
long before
our children dream
of walking across
a graduation stage
of any strata
or down the aisle
of their unlikely wedding.
We give birth to
casket pretty babies
that are the closest thing
in this delphinium world
to the walking dead.

Black Like Me

Little niggas
with more heart
than Jesus,

sport big ass pistols
through America
the free, this land
of crosses swaying
in our incandescent nights,

or so you might think
lowly bystanders on the street
corners, or snuck away
in the alleys,
each undoubtedly with
a cellphone to record tragedy,

as well as the cops,
heroes, vigilantes,
and plain ol'-fashioned
murderers too,

that will make a
man, a boy, a
child, hell, any Black body,
a martyr tonight,
and tomorrow night,
and the night after that,
and every moon-brightened moment onwards,
that Black flesh still breathes.

Mirror of a Mirror

I cannot quell this sense
that I failed my brother.

As children, my older brother told me
that his handwriting was
so small and pretty,
to me
his letters flew like gulls
afar on the horizon,
because that was how he
hid from his teachers.

I laughed at his absurdity.
Why would you hide from
people paid to teach you?

We were adults when I
learned of his dyslexia,
of how he, the peacock,
hid age-old festering wounds
with emerald feathers he
had meticulously preened his whole life.

My brother, the beautiful one,
was a dysfunctional husk
of all I had known of him,
truly odd and pathetic
like I was, vulnerable
like I was, but by then
it was too late.

For too long, I echoed
the lies he told me about himself—
how free he was, how bold he was,
until I was blind to the cruelty he would suffer,
as well as the cruelty he would inflict.

I did not truly see you, helion wonder, all your life,
my glorious mirror of opposing virtue,
and when you were undone, I was undone.

White Death Cocoon

Hospital intensive care rooms are moon-white cloisters
where dying patients wane ever so violently
and then vanish as if all at once.
Seven years ago, my father, my pastor,
disappeared also. His HIV-related stroke
made him a fat, black, drooling eggplant,
swathed in white. Even years after he heard
Jesus' call, he still refused to confess
his ten-year-plus HIV diagnosis to anyone.
I only learned because the hospital's head ethicist
had to tell me, making removing him from life support
much easier. I prayed his secret, his death,
and my decision would finally collapse
that alabaster slaughterhouse,
and stain it with rainbows, but the room,
having already known so many deaths,
remained as before.

One Night

There was one night
that proved all suspicions
of things heinous,
human, and silently consented.

Walking into
darkness, a young man
sees his father sitting
at a computer screen.

It wasn't the sight of anything,
just quickness of gesture
so familiar to the boy
with its atmosphere
of delphinium shame.

No judgment
issues from the mouth
of the young man who could call disgrace
back to God where it
blossomed long ago.

Both actors emerge
from the mise-en-scène
with the same crime coating
their hands at one time
or another, but with a clear
difference expressed
in the privileges known.

One was just becoming a young man then,
while the other had been a man for a while.
Worthless was the title
gained by the father's monstrous
child, from the father's own lips,
if the son should not
decline the need of
interventions and exorcisms,
not in response of
deed, but in the
 nature of its
inspiration—

when roles were reversed,
frozen on the boy's computer screen
were muscles turning slow as the moon,
accented by moans of ecstasy,
and sweat, nectar drunk
from the dimpled hips
of floaty young Ganymede
multiplied and differentiated,
fulfilling taste across the racial spectrum.

A Train and a Funeral

I had to hop a train
to bury my most recent dead.

His body laid up in the funeral home
at the other side of the tracks.

I parked my car
in the liquor store parking lot
after having raced
one hundred miles under a clear sky
from Orangeburg to Charleston
to see another slain Black boy
dressed some type of way
in a coffin, dressed
by his mama one last,
for eternal sleep.

I had arrived just as the funeral
was hoppin' to,
just as my sister's head wrap
and mother's hijab came into sight
behind the scattered limousines
and various cars that
encircled the funeral parlor,
perfumed center, cusped by
the outer petals of a
newly bloomed moon white rose.

I didn't want to be
that nigga who acted fool,
so I hesitated for a few moments

thinking I could just wait
or drive along until I could discover
a more respectable way across,
like I had that kind of time.

But then the youth,
friends of my murdered cousin,
in their late teens
and early twenties
started walking towards the train,
entirely unrestrained by respectability politics,

and so I, newly inspired,
walked with them,
and as we approached
and saw that even climbing
a still train is cumbersome,
they devised their strategies.

But once I heard a girl
suggest climbing under a stopped train
that could foreseeably start again
at any time, I threw my leg
on a high bar, and reached
for bars that were even higher,
and hoisted myself to every
foothold that I could see

and leaped down and crossed
a ditch like I was a kid again
doing the long jump at a track meet
to see this young man be put
with the rest of our chthonic kin.

Georgia Ex-Con

Brotha, in your younger days,
you threw dope to the youngins,
mirroring old folks tossing bread to swans
and came up with dollas
yet still was nigga po'
'cause what ripped through their bodies
did not rip through your own.

You got a bad hand in high school
catching a ride with ya' lil white "friends"
who stole guns from country trailers on the low
'cause they thought they had a good buyer
and it was an easy job,
but you got caught up with them and sold out,
the lone Black boy,
the only one convicted,
for a crime you didn't even commit.

You went away for years
into a forbidden city
not an ancient palace of colored wood, but of cement
and similarly armed guards

of rapists (the rare ones
they could catch and
successfully prosecute)
and murderers (some,
exonerated by
DNA evidence after
a fifty-year separation
from the world)

in the days when your baby cried out
and shed tears for the first time,
but now, you not so young no mo',
brother, what will you do with yourself?

When I was Little

and still held fondness
toward outside play,
where tree climbing
meant speaking
with the woodpecker's
holes and making
wrinkled tree flesh

into a lover's torso—
pressing hands
and sometimes genitals
against viscous trails of golden blood—
I ate azaleas with my older brother.

We ruthlessly snatched the flowers
from their branches,
our cruel facsimile
of tearing legs
off writhing toads.
We stole the sweet nectar
into our mouths
beneath an untroubled sky
to drug ourselves
into the state of lunar gods.

Petals were torn apart
while inspecting
their miniature
pink cheetah spots
and mashed beneath

our feet into a dirty paste
of pink and brown.

We stuck the bottoms
of the stamens
into our mouths,
pretending that they were

toothpicks. And as pollen
peppered our upper lips,
We seduced the monarchs.

Tangerine

When the church is silent,
the devil has come,
so says my father, the preacher man.
He might say...
that ol' devil has come
and robbed you children of the word;
he snipped your tongues
out so that you might not confess,
so that you do not offer testimony;
he sealed your eyelids with melted gold
to make you sightless;
he weighed your limbs down
with the stiffness of death,
so that you might not throw
your hands up in fervor, or let loose
your dancing feet in celebration.

But suddenly the silence breaks,
and the preacher man wonders
what finally sent the devil out.

He looks out along the
sea of faces, each touched
by melanin in their own way,
from cotton to obsidian glass,
and accepts it wasn't his sweet,
jazzy, delphinium words,
the choir's mechanical, gospel singing,
the wailing of the bored and hungry babies,
the hum of incessant overhead fans,

but the thud of a plastic tangerine,
set free from a bouquet of plastic fruit
lining the rim of an old,
Black woman's indigo crown,
a most majestic sun at dawn
come just in time
to send away a moonless night.

Garland of Delphinium

What happens when a young man,
a caramel-colored step-cousin,
you've kissed (not on the mouth)
and fondled in the nighttime

is shot?

You grew up together,
but did not end up together.
He had children,
but you have none.

He became a man
and you did too.
But what of
the fruits of your labors?
What of the young
grapes of your dreams
that turned sour on the vine?
Twenty-eight was the age

my brother got killed.
Why can't that also
be the age that my
first true lover
transmogrifies into
the silt that
moon-making oysters
coat into lustrous,
soft, blue pearls?

Why can't that be
the age where
I too become a noose
of delphinium hung
from an oak tree?
Why do I still fear
to join their
boyish footrace
to their graves?

City by the Sea

Days before 2019
rolls in, I find myself
driving around
my grandfather,
so that he can play
his lotto. I've never driven in Florida,
in Port Saint Lucie,
and my first time driving these streets
as a new, black missing moon
is at night, beside this
dark-skinned, little Jamaican American man.

Two places we've gone to
are already closed.
It's at the third
that I am reminded
of one of the many reasons
why I don't like Florida

(in Miami Dade County,
my uncle, Frisco Blackwood,
and his friend were both twenty-one years old
when police shot and killed them
with nearly thirty bullets racing through my uncle's SUV,
as the young lady in
the backseat, also with a bullet
lodged in her supple thigh,
prayed in the language
of the black swans to be
spared, and strangely,

God heard her swan song,
and that darling angel, Death, refused her the touch,
passing the young girl over, such that she lived,
five years before Trayvon Martin would be murdered by a vigilante)

and why I don't like
to be out in the world at night

(because the three murder victims I've known and loved,
my uncle, my brother, and my cousin, were all slain
with glorious mother Nyx dancing on the streets
and her radiant daughter, Hemera, absent in her bed).

When we enter
the gas station my grandfather
heads to the counter
for a pencil and
a white woman walks up to tell my grandfather,
"I'm going ahead of you."

There are only two
Black people here—
my grandfather and I.
The cashier is a white man
who acquiesces to this
white woman's presence,
And then there is this white woman herself.

She drunkenly scuttles her
way in front of him.
He seems as if he is about
to say something as the woman asks him:
"Where ya' from?"

"You an island boy?"

My grandfather,
a man in his eighties,
is a boy to a woman
who may be half his age
or a little more at most.

Then to deepen
an already grievous wound,
she speaks a drunken,
butchered, patois to him.

Midnight: Paradise of Self

(M)others, (W)omen

When I was five
I thought that if
I prayed hard enough
that God would give
me a baby, a mirror
moon of my very own
like my mother.

I thought I knew
a boy would have
to kiss me, to
touch me in
the delphinium places
that were most often
mine alone to
summon this child
into being, but

I did not know
then of the elements
that would deny me
of my wish—

1) I couldn't get pregnant
at five. Bodies typically
refuse such requests.

2) Boys can't be mothers.
Who knew?

To Teach New Love

Into a field I go,
dragging a circle
bound by olive branches,
and creeping darkness from the unseen portion of the moon.

Hecate,
the she-wolf,
the three-faced guard,
the torch of hallowed graves
with power
of the earthen words,
the path of stars,
malicious gestures,
sleeping
and the killing
charms—
I beseech you.

Work your insidious arts in the witching hour.
Force shadows up
from the blue underworld
and send them adrift
with hooked chains
of silver and gold to torment
and ensnare all hearts.

Make them split open in ecstasy
and feed their new gaping mouths
and aching lips
viscous morning out

of the greatest goblet of the cupbearer,
accented with petals of delphinium and Narcissus's flower.
Make the world the refuge of N. vengeance,
of the house of N.

Make the world sing madly
of forbidden, strange fruits that fed deader epochs,
screaming from pages of history.

Make the world all loves,
chanted amongst the hungry ghosts,
jackals of the golden sands,
and winged monstrosities
gracing new heavens, praising a master also of three.

We

How early is
a queer child born?
Sometimes, we know ourselves
as young as four,
dreaming

of the most
artless, red, wet kisses,
the brushing together
of bare, scabbed kneecaps,
or dry, naked elbows,
or even the insignificant
rubbing of pinkies.

It is these
osculates of desire,
these fragments
of misguided innocence
and la petite mort,
which we cobble
together with
our monstrous,
infantile fingers,
and solidify
with the glue
of our polymorphous perversity,
as rough-edged,
Azul jewels of love,

beneath the slide,
or up high,
climbing on a green mossy oak,
or down low,

wrestling, as if
for blessings
from alabaster, lunatic angels,
in the mud,
at the sandbox,
or on nap-time mats,
just before eyes
grow heavy
and our best secrets are softly whispered.

Underemployed While Being a Black American

Working as a cashier
while being Black
teaches you a few things,
but none so important as this:
people assume you've done nothing
with your life because of the job you have.
My saving grace is my piquant wit.
But before I can speak, I
must be spoken to.
I must be acknowledged as an equal.

Without my Heidegger,
Milton, Ellison, Aristotle,
Flaubert, Faulkner, and Morrison,
I would have no shield,
being merely a Black body thought
to have no brain, and thus
a lesser soul.

No customer with any real money
in their pocket, of any color or creed,
gives the benefit of the doubt that
someone like me might be cultured,
might have a sensitivity
to matters of a higher aesthetic,
might be someone a little bit more complicated,
without those books either being in my hands,
or constantly near the register.

And so a lesson I learned quite early as a child

aids me well in presenting my humanity
to the masses that I must accommodate:
To be an intellectual,
I must carry the articles of an intellectual,
and then and only then
can I astound, as nappy hair
and moonless, dark, Black skin,
almond eyes, and full lips,
rightfully become
the opulent embodiment
of a fervent autodidacticism
and unconquerable will.

Fallen Child

Where is the world?
The earth beneath,
the sky above,
and I was in between.
Pigeons, crows, and other
feathered treasures fly through clouds
of simple sky, delphinium,
soft, cotton soft, that azure horizon.
And I looked to see where my wings were.
The park, the fountain,
and always the birds with their
Fluttering wings,
Little hurricanes,
Little murderers.

Crows and pigeons,
messengers and saints of Black like me.
Where were my wings?
Where were my feathers
that touch brother sun,
that touch mother earth,
and touch me, mirror moon?

Where were my feathers
decorated with secret
flecks of rose, streaks of violet, and splashes of scarlet,
the plumage of so much succulent flesh?

Come see,
as I search for
my wings.
My wings,
my wings!

with bones broken,
body gnarled
Ah yes, I fell through the
Blue. the cotton clouds
were empty wisps of cold wind and ice.
How alive I am, finally, as a falling legend with the dead.

Don't Call Me Middle Class

I don't see how
someone looks at me
and musters the gall
to say that I am middle class;

I am clothed in blue-
Black skin here in the
United States of America
with childhood memories
of sewer rats on stoves
with blood-red eyes,
and roaches that
called from open garbage,
desperate whispers
of a delphinium sea.

And an adolescence
with scenes of
my brother preparing
weed in my grandmother's
Victorian house
to sell somewhere,
and the return of roaches
to the little azure house where
my father and his dead wife lived,
crawling over plastic
in the night mimicking
the heavenly song of rain,

and finally my adulthood

where I have two college degrees,
but no job, and still
the close presence of
roaches, though much
more infrequent in their appearances—
surprising apparitions of the moonless dark
who make no sound at all.

Lonely Song

Two lips,
tulips,
briefly
brush soft against
each other in
a spring breeze,
with a spring ease,
fleeing Zephyrus's
delphinium blessing.

And I, the second-born son,
sit amongst stars, Earth's lonely moon.
My mother, her lone daughter,
her murdered first-born too,
we all sit with no companion,
to trust nor love as we deserve
at this moment.

Tulips, like always,
lose the rhythm
of their master,
scatter,
separated, into
quiet darkness, into mud

like we four—
mother, daughter,
dead son, live one.

Go with the Flesh

Go with the flesh and become like delphinium.
Lay with the brown serpents in the fields of tall grass.
Remove the skin and live the dirtier freedoms.

Return home. It no longer accepts masters.
Your heart has come to stillness.
Its orifices, starved, then ravaged dead.
What of the lower gods resting with our Lord?

The child called Mercy burns with her broken mirror upon a lonely pyre.
The child called Patience is crucified by her sycophantic pretenders.
The child called Empathy wears her noose of bitter rose thorns.

God, with his matted locks, and moon-drunk eyes,
wept stones, but turned his ebony face and said nothing.
His ruby rivers ceased. He looks for us no more.

Maybe I'll Win

Who can open the heavy doors of success?

Though metaphor, they seem more sturdy
than any door of iron and mammoth oak.

The answer is—
none, but those who hold the fabled "keys"
(of gold, diamond
and mother of pearl, elaborately constituted,
and worshiped by obsequious idolaters)

or rarer,
those who've left the one antediluvian secret
written on yellowed paper,
solitary moon that it is, in its own terrible loneliness,
woven so delicately around rusted hinges.

And the secret,
what's always written,
not always with the same words, or language,
but always with the same cruel love,
with the same expeditious hands,
eager to forget groveling and prayers
is the phrase "maybe this time."

or rarest of all, the tenderhearted,
the lunatic, or the dimwitted
who've left the door ajar,
an inch at best, a crack
with the song of the western wind
sung just for you, like a horn,
to remind you what they've done.

A Snake Takes Flight

if i wasn't born with a black storm in my black body, i would have chosen
to live thus far instead with dawn crying out inside of me —a bursting
ulcer of a morning, a morning of all the fruits of red, fuchsia, and gold.
i would've spoken languages, human & otherwise, conversing with my
neighbors like they were exactly what they are, people my life might one
day depend upon, blessed strangers, and other mysterious beings who might
also share that burden of salvation, hyenas, doves, lions, tulips, trumpets,
and manticores amongst them. i would've talked to them all without my
forked tongue, unafraid, open with sun fire, warm, and loving. i would've
danced in the dark with my mirror, the moon, every night i could breathe
and find my feet. i would've surrounded myself with delphinium, and
redheaded opium poppies every day and drink rum-rich sorrel with my
jamaican grandfather and his first wife, my dead grandmother, whom i've
never met too. god would've loved me already, wish god would love me
already, wish god would love me, if only, if only, if only:

_____. i would've
already lived as a big-eyed, longhaired, dark-skinned black boy wearing a
dress in some oasis in the sahara, in full bloom, sweet with date palms, and
my dress would caress my thighs while i spun in circles beside the sufis, but
inspired by and meditating upon much different matters in my dancing. i
would be more than mother, more than father, i would be trinity—i would
be love, discipline, and creativity. i would roll down verdant hills and sing
at the top of my strong lungs, tuneless and unashamed. i would've been
born my greatest love, my greatest creation, and shared that love as often as
i could. if i was born with wings like my siblings, i would've kissed someone
by now, become gooey honey, and felt my lover melt with me. though i am
missing parts, maybe someone one day might share theirs and let me soar
up off my belly. take me into the sky, my future love, so that i might soar
with heaven still on my back and even the darkest storm inside of me could
not conquer the grace of venus, light bearer, our luciferous morning drop.

From Up on High

In the scale of Goliath,
I did fall, bested—
the reversal of David's
fortune, I did
fall, my own version of Icarus's
delphinium ruin, with the melted
wax and feather wings
of my precious ego.

I did fall—
from the University of Chicago
with its life of the mind
bred by a pantheon of intellectual dynamos
nestled in their ivory towers,
nestled so close to the bosom
of Mnemosyne
and the nine Muses,

and sequestered away from Cottage Grove
and the 'hoods of the Southside
like a pearl cloistered away
from the black, turbulent sea

I fell and now
I try to find my way
along a moonless path—
efforts too that are mythic,
herculean in their difficulty,
Sisyphean in their repetitiveness—
get money

pay bills
keep a roof
over my head.

Seven Chthonic Lessons I Learned from the Mandibles of Worms at My Father's Grave

The soil of a fresh dug grave is dark and wet,
but once the grave is filled, it shines with moons and stars,
the night sky residing there too.

The living fill their days with prayers and pleas,
but learn only too late that those
who beg for love are least likely to get it.

All men are delphinium gardens of garish machinations,
since they've been swaddled by fear since their suckling days,
and they believe the world owes each a debt of much suffering.

Failure is always manifesting itself
as the truth of man's reality— a flat
earth, planets revolving in perfect circles,
the earth at the center and not the sun.

Man never considers that there are richer
voices in the night—the hoot of the owl and
the howl of the wolf—than there are at dawn.

When humans cut down the oak of their own wisdom,
an act done often with great fervor,
all they end up with is the yoke of their own undoing.

The living are tired all the time because
they are diseased with dispassion, but once they
come to the grave, we worms will eat away that corruption,
and such appetites will be born.

When Might Dark Skin Be Loved?

One day—Hemera,
night, Queen Nyx,
divine airs, merge,
becoming
eternal moonless night,
destructively loves
the earth
becoming
perpetual
darkness,
with
only the
comfort

of distant
quiet stars,
standing eternally
united, as offerings
for the people
their quixotic hope
as slow echoes,
the dark body
sacred living temples
known as
African-descended flesh,
perpetual martyrs,
citizens of all

Love, transforms into
that illustrious ichor,
as sable flesh
together as
that which only
comes to
pass
when
both divine airs,
day and night
and intermingled progeny,
who surely
are as vanquished.

Ritual of the Lonely-Hearted

I sought the soul of another
and for that, I had to pay a price
so I cast my soul into a mirror
and the mirror took it.
My soul left my sable flesh
behind for the camera
so that my reflection
could angle itself for
the art of seduction.

My reflection
made its waist slim
by relinquishing
all of its breath.
My reflection tightened
its muscles from head
to toe. My reflection
turned so that its
dark face caught the false moonlight.
My reflection positioned
its shoulders back
and pushed its chest out.
After a little fondling,
it allowed a long, veiny erection
to stargaze, though
the thick, upright child was
of a clan of sable Cyclopes born
with a hollow, an empty socket,
missing its instrument
of oppressive sight.

And once my reflection
was immortalized in
its arousal, its image
flew to the internet
so that it might finally
be baptized in the delphinium gaze
of thousands of men,
so that the image might
trap the beating heart of one,
so that it might find a second soul,
a second soul that might take residence
in the husk of me.

Moon Shadow

Scarab black, in
a public school,
on a list,
of a list,
somewhere both
distant and near—

I was a student,
then a teacher,
then a nigga
with no job.
What did I
learn from these
changing states?

Am I still intelligent?
Can I speak at length
on the contemplation
of beauty that
Toni Morrison explores
in The Bluest Eye?
Of course, but
would anyone listen?

As a student who once
paid to be heard—
voices erupted constantly,
but not for my sake,
and most definitely
not for my instructor's.

No one heard anyone
in the classroom
though many spoke.

As a teacher who
was paid to speak—
I yelled at my garden
of rebellious delphinium blooms
and they felt the fire
of my tired, worn-out breath,
but heard none of
the wit of my words,
and they were stunted
and annoyed that
I wasted their playtime,
which was always.

And as a nigga
with no job, I
lay about, an
unwanted house cat, purring
into an empty apartment,
bemused by the
symphony of my
self-imposed solitude.

Don't nobody want
to hear nothing
from a nigga
with no job
most of all.

We

are the shadows of planets
and moons—
perpetually ignorable,
except on the rarest of occasions
where darkness outdazzles light.

Don't Be Like Me

Fuck.
Suck.
Rage and run.
Blow your brains out
with self-love.

Fight your mother,
fight your father,
fight your obnoxious
pimps, whoring you out
for peasant profits.

Flee from abuse and call
it what it is—
the traps of love.

Masturbate your way
into delphinium
Nirvana/Oblivion,
juxtaposing
perfectly
perversity
and piety.

And as you walk
conflicting paths,
of heroin addicts
and sodomites,
of ascetics
and nuns,

cultivate
kindness
exceeding
the pure.

Be the unloved child
of these diverging bloodlines
and reveal the great folly
of sinners and saints alike.

Towards Midnight

I'm a dark child from a dark world
somewhere out there from beyond the waters,
a fleet-footed ghost now hiding amongst delphinium
eating the gristle of a raccoon's spine,
begging God, please let me be free

and out of my eyes
flow diamonds
tinged with blood
and when those tears bless the earth,

I cough up bolts of lightning
while atop a kitchen table,
an altar, a humble stump out in the swamps,
where prayers are carved
by hands forced to pluck the whitest clouds,

and my forked blessings of
Zeus / Yahweh / Olodumare / Whomever the good goddamn
that crack through the sky
force past to parley with present
as sunshine converts
into pooling purples
and inky blacks
and my dark moon face
is hidden by a deluge
of scarlet viscera, willingly freed up
from suiciding manticores, unicorns, griffons,
leviathans, and freedom, sacrosanct wonders that never were.

Duende

Nobody loves the angel
or the muse, like they
love my nigga, the duende.

The duende
be that genius child
who is like me,
to everyone's surprise,
with a crown, not of laurel or gold,
but of woolly kinks
and sharpest curls.

My nigga
the duende
draws Promethean
flame out from the blood
and ancient earth
and shares it with
the kids who've
met the fire before
in dream
and delphinium baptism.

The duende be
that nigga,
that dark miracle,
who loves me
in all of my Black wonder
and leaves me
in all of my Black wonder
and comes back again

with the sound of drums
and dusty Black feet,
smiling in my face, flashing luminous
pearls fished from the deep,
to coax away the righteous fury
this nigga inspired by his
continuous abandonment of me,
innocently smiling, in his returns,
as if we've just met,
just known each other,
for the first time.

My nigga duende loves to dance
through the desert of my mind
where it's always night
and I follow him into the darkness,
wherever he may go.

And when we dance in the desert,
we dance with the luciferous moon,
the wise neon serpents,
and the spinning flowers.

Then the duende goes again
away from me
and I wait for him
to come again
and play with me
and love me
like he did before.

Choices of Mine

I am eaten
by the wolves
that I invited
into my own
moon-drenched abode,
into my house
of wrathful heathen worship.

Over plates,
broken and scattered
they leap,
onto beds, they tussle,
bespeckled by their fleas,

and wallow amongst
my dirty clothes
strewn about my carpeted floor.

These greedy wildlings
have had their way
and trot so calmly
out my door

with dazzling
red grins
caked with gore
and the smell
of withered delphinium
rolling deep
in the backs of
their throats.

Childhood Grace

Hyenas dance
in my memories
twisting and leaping
in our childhood play,
their swift paws
barely pressing into
the dry, red, flowing dust.

laughing at my frailty—

Little blue-Black boy,
marvelous dark lunatic,
starved baby vulture
that I was, has come to some peace
with my skin, a hide painted by a bath of soot
from a funeral pyre
that clings to my body, now more beloved than despised,
more beautiful than grotesque, my skin, my shining obsidian armor,
a blessed child of God in its own right like any other.

I remember still what
it means to be
so unlike the others,
with my eyes
so owlish,
moon-worshipping,

holding a gaze widened
full, shining, while
always secretly watching

the dark, lit by
the fire of the gas heater
where I slumbered,
for my dream, a lover who would come
and snatch me away

from my banal affairs
with the sewer rats and roaches,
and the dime bags
in the front yard,
used condoms in the back,
and the holes in
the ceilings and floors
of my ruined domicile.

Luciferous Child

My mother gave birth to me just like she gave birth to my brother, but before his vicious murder, he was a shoe that the world wore all kinds of places, and I have strived all my life to lay claim to my identity as a book, in a library somewhere, longing to be read. My brother was a shoe, and I am becoming something, but I am most likely a book. I hope I am a book. Let me be anything other than a gun. We look human, my brother and I. We look human, and we are, we are, we are, even if not to everyone, but we are also not human, especially him, especially now, being a beautiful mahogany corpse. My brother is a corpse now, filled with stitched-up bullet wounds, buried deep in the dark rich soil of South Carolina, in our ancestral burial ground of Shad, if he is still even that. He had hair, skin, eyes, scars, breath, boogers, blood, bile, shit, piss, and tears, tears, tears while he was alive, though his Black body shed tears the least. Now he may only have bones left to him that can't even rattle in his tight, friendless coffin.

What are Black boys when the world does not love us as boys, but as instruments? Parents can only do so much for children that are not children to the world, but tools. Things, human things. Inhuman things. We are things. We are things. We are things. We are flesh, and also objects. So what is a Black boy really? Is he an instrument of fire? Is he a loathsome gun perhaps? Is he a hot spoon? Is he a bale of blood-soaked cotton? Is he a primrose, a cipher, delphinium blessed by a bath of moonlight, a gold-besieged honeycomb, a fleshy avatar of Steatopygian Eros? We Black boys can be all these marvels, but in our hidden place, made first amongst the oldest things, a Black boy is always already a desert rose of Jericho, if we live, like Orpheus, Osiris, and the Nazarene before us. Like them, we Black boys must survive journeys through continents of bone, dark cities of blood, and terrible oceans of viscera, like they did, and come back from the other side of the veil, like they did, even if partly claimed by the dark jewels of the pomegranate, like Queen Persephone wedded to ebon Hades. We must do that herculean task, and always come back from the dead, or else be an eternal bride to the recherché deity, like all the other shades in his somnolent abode.

And

I don't need folks to tell me
what I ain't got.

I got two degrees,
no student loan debt,
and no children I can't afford to feed.

I also got nobody
to warm my bed beside me.

No boyfriend,
no girlfriend,
nobody of any kind.

I got no love left to give
'cause my cold, lonely
moon of a heart has gone empty
and become a diamond shell,

buried somewhere, like my stepmother,
my brother, and my father before me.

Now all I wait for, all I want is
the barren winter when I too might join them,
songless in the unyielding soil.

I Hope to Be Given

In my coffin
leave delphinium
and apples.
Let them rot
down with me.

Let their
seeds be
nourished
with decay

and let me
rise up towards
the moon anew.
Let me become
the apple tree.

Poor me don't
want nothing else,
can't want nothing else—

those that have nothing
have no room for
sentimentality,
not even in the grave.

I am the Lady Cassandra

I sit with voices
everyday that sing
the chorus of swarming
bees in my bloated cranium.
And the voices, vast in
their wisdoms, are always
a variation of my husky tone.

And so I have made
my attempts to
give them form
and bring them along
out of antediluvian
wine dark seas of creation—
as poems,
stories, essays,
dialogues, and soliloquies,
as carvings in sacred oaks
and stones, matters that
masquerade as eternal things,
as sigils for those
initiated into mystery cults.

They are the prophecies
of empires and all that
is of them, the fates
of despots, priests,
philosophers, magicians,
martyrs, kings, and

my older brother, Hector,
murdered then, as he is
murdered now
being a Black corpse
of a different name
in a different glorious city
that served as both
cradle and grave.

But what should I
want, care for, or believe?
I am the lady Cassandra
of doomed Troy,
stuck in my boy body
of bodies, victim
of a god's cruel love,
in my temple
of temples that I've
tried to worship at many times
and always failed.

I am immortalized
and reincarnated always
the birther of panoptic visions
of horrors and woes denied—
a dumbwaiter still delivering
spoiled meat, rotten eggs, and
wine turned to vinegar
to all my beloveds.

And no one can find me
and whisper the truths
I need to cease this madness

because the great vision of man,
like the gaze of the single-eyed progeny
of Poseidon, is easily blinded
and the three, the Moirai,
Clotho, the tome,
Lachesis, the television,
Atropos, the oracular ghost,
artificial intelligence,
ordered reality blinded
to me and my body's insights—

soon black miracles will reign
down from heaven again
and Black bodies will
drop down here on earth,
dead, so loveless, and abandoned,
in as many scenarios that
the mind can imagine, but
this time, the world will
weep for the dead Black children
and be slow to decide if it's alright
to look away now that
the horror is finally believed
by everyone with and
without eyes to see,
ears to hear,
fingers that touch,
and hearts that feel.

Moonset: Resurrecting Social Worlds

A Lesson Henrietta Lacks Teaches Anyone
Willing to Learn

Debate personhood all you like stranger,
just as the menfolk who deny those who seek
autonomy over their own bodies,
but ask yourself this first—
why shouldn't womb
bearers destroy life?

In every flesh born is a world of souls, trillions of souls.
In every flesh is a world of trillions of deaths.
What difference does the method of death
or the timing make before the countless lives perpetually lost?

Every single being that has and will ever exist
is a unique Bible unto themselves and undeniably equal in their holiness—
the creatures of the sea, the fowl of the air,
and all manner of things that scurry above and below the soil,
like dear Mrs. Henrietta Lacks, dead of cervical cancer since 1951,
even as her cells proliferate ad infinitum to this day
outside her one and only Black corpse
without her consent,
or the consent of her children,
or the consent of her grandchildren,
or the consent of her great-grandchildren,
and so forth and so on in labs across the world,

or your baby that cried,
the silent, unrecognizable clump of cells
it once was, the sperms that didn't survive
their programmed journeys in wombs

across reality,
the eggs that will go on
unfertilized to degeneration
and death.

Is not all flesh
Genesis and Revelations,
and everything between?

All deaths, from the death of an amoeba,
to the death of a blue whale,
is the death of God, souls, and realities.

Building the Great Work

Only once did the people of this world
understand each other
or rather only once did they
collectively suffer under the illusion
of understanding—
the darker-skinned, copper-toned, olive-tinted, and snow-white.

They brought themselves to work together,
beneath the mirthful sun, beneath the somber moon, as diligently as mindless ants,
with their hoes, and their shovels, and their woeful beasts of burden,
birthing music into this world with the orchestra of their percussional labors—
rocks and lumps of dirt scattering from the peaks of freshly turned piles of soil,
water pouring into troughs filled with sand, lime, and pulverized stone,
rods pinging against the sides of massive vats, as they stir frothy mortar,
heavy sculpted blocks baking in ovens amongst crazed, roaring flames,
mortar sucking on fresh-baked bricks as they are gently pressed into place,
and finally the scraping away of excesses, with fingers and thin wooden planks,
as mortar dries upon brick.

And as these great sounds coupled with little sounds,
as foreign and familiar tongues echoed the same symbols,
as brick stacked upon brick,
their fusion was cemented by a singular pride,
contributed by an amoeba of a man,
or a collective of men, seemingly aligned in their ambitions,
as is often recorded, always
faceless and unaccountable, faceless and unquestionable,
faceless and unpunishable

completely removed from the slavish labors performed on behalf
of a monument—
a phallic monument
commissioned to celebrate
industry, commerce, and innovation,
a phallic monument
commissioned to celebrate
union, equality, and humanity,
but most truly a monument
to the frail illusion of human strength:
in the manipulation of the citizen,
in the sacrifice of individual sovereignty,
controlling blood, and bone, and hands
and tongue and the one language
that appeared to be the site
of belonging and understanding.
But as with all great cities, and all great monuments,
so the tower was destroyed, and the great language
confounded, but the pride that fused them together
flowered anew amongst the scattering multitude
with their method of knowing Elohim
rethought and vastly multiplied.

Swim Swim

I am liquored up
and high as Venus
'cause I can't
be sober before
this beautiful boy
who precariously
decided to
kiss me—

with his lips
so full like
finely sautéed shrimp,
and his fiery
tongue, swollen
with vodka
and other dangerous
miracles that have
survived the march
of history.

Through the
ocean of narcotics,
not milk, must I
travel to have
what I so desperately want.

Through the delphinium
ocean of libations
am I baptized
so that I

may have the
mercy of lunar gods
and what I need—

acknowledgment
from the hands,
and mouth, and
other things,
of this heavenly
daemon, this

wild thing,
this garish moon
begging for me
to pluck it from
its majestic perch,
aloof and drifting
towards heaven
in the greedy,
starry sky
before me.

Soon Only Electric Sleep

In a couple of years,
America will consist of generations
never privy to the use of an outhouse.

It will be a land
where there are
no more stories
of checking for snakes
hidden by a moonless night
once the midnight urges
set feet shuffling
over hardwood then grass,
intestines churning
and wiggling or
bladder swishing,
gushing, and bursting.

There will only be memories
of clean, white, porcelain thrones,
stationed atop mazes of lead
and other metal piping.

There will be no more stories
of long violet nights
with only the great white moon,
chartreuse fireflies,
scattered stars,
and a kerosene lamp.

In America today,

there is already no such thing as
night, darkness, or silence.
There is no escaping
the hum and glow of electricity.

In a couple of years,
from plague, or simply time, America will be—
only electric memories, electric stories, and electric dreams—
and after long enough, the world.
One day, nobody will remember the before times.

With Your Own Eyes Believe

Remember your faith,
like Schrodinger' cat,
both dead and alive,
that estranged quagmire,
that conundrum
breeding circuitous realities.
It is not your flesh.
It is removed, defenestrated
and made nomadic, wandering
mystified by concentric spheres
of opulent, holy firmament.

Your faith bears witness
to gilded seraphim
serpentine fingers
coiling cruelly above
your collar. Providence
asphyxiates you.

But still, value the promise of belief,
as disembodied love,
our fastidious, luminary lord,
the omnipotent ethereal,
orbits planes not forlorn.

It envelopes itself with attendants
of marigold tendrils, whose
flesh is the plume of albino
peacocks, moon white, with desert
rosette eyes of fluorescent beige, unlike

the attendants' own uncountable
eyes of electric, delphinium blue,
their multiracial veiling undeniably absent.

Two Pairs of Black Lips

Into a bowl of water,
into a bowl of salt,
I birthed a secret

consecrated by blood
of my mouth
that required
a miniature
cerulean sea to cleanse
and make whole again.

I kissed a boy who
responded with his
tongue for a moment
and then his fist for
a long time.

My blood was
so rich with iron
that I thought I
must be a
statue underneath.

I had to be something else
than simply this
brown-eyed,
lunatic,
mahogany-skinned imp,
who stole a kiss from
another Black boy,

and never once
said sorry, but
begged God even
as he punched my skull
with his brick knuckles,
please let me have one kiss more.

Churches of Hemlock

Victorian looming columns
of moon white,
chiseled blue whale bones,
stand tall, holding up
the roofs of nightmarish houses
filled with Black feet,
and Black hands,
Black backs,
and Black arms, severed
and stitched back together
into a blasphemous cathedral
of unbridled suffering.

These laughable temples
hold the ghosts of letters that
were forbidden from being read,
house nigger gossip and worries,
and field nigger terrors of the bullwhip
and still more trepidations than even these.

Such sacred places
consecrated by
massacre, exploitation,
and denial

are wandered
by free bodies
that know not
the fierce kiss
of bondage.

Do you think
they weep, or at
least remember correctly
they walk a land of agony?

It's foolish to believe this country would be like this
if folks recalled our collective history correctly, so no.
They take pretty pictures, and have pretty weddings,
loving houses still imbued with the most unspoken
miseries of the long since dead,
whose many descendants, a diaspora of delphinium, moon vine, scarlet oleander,
and strange fruit, still tragically become horrific garlands of the trees sometimes,
while others, much more frequently, are made into decorations of the streets.

#OregonUnderAttack

I can stand
gun in hand,
as part of one of many
white male domestic militias

and occupy a federal building
in the state of Oregon,
home of the beloved
white holy land
that is Portland,

but whisper nary a word
about how dead Black bodies
of all ages litter television sets daily
or how the U.S. government
keeps brown children in cages,
unwashed, underfed, with babies
desperately watching over even younger babies,
and all of them sleeping in filth on concrete floors,
or how children of every shade are butchered by guns
in any place that they might find themselves.

I am the greedy beloved child God so favors.
I gleefully march with death machines
in government facilities unscathed, ceaselessly invoking
the ravenous lunatic angels of patriotism and nationalism,
long nursed on the cadavers created
from America's many systematic hecatombs.
I am the original American wraith,
of pulchritudinous delphinium, scarlet oleander, and moon vine

of both past and present, crying out anew.

I appear again, unhidden
by the hood and regalia of old,
to tell all of America's
melanin-kissed, lesser-loved progeny
I am here to take back my rightful pride,
my pure, heterosexual flesh,
and my bountiful land,
that I earned by bloodshed,
and will keep by bloodshed,
"by any means necessary",
so help me God.

The Fair

House of mirrors—

                                        a train of loveless people.

          House of horrors—

               a delphinium world with "love" in it.

               Tunnel of "love"—
               Mirrors in mirrors in mirrors.

Sadhana in the Public Library

click, clack, clap, ring—
pencils, cellphones, keyboards, pages,
loudly screech a homely chorus
in a house once known
for belle lettres and quietude,
silent temples of the moon where
Woolf, Joyce, and Shakespeare's
immortal forms reside.

Most silent in the library
are japa mala beads
of yellow, green, red, brown
passing delicately
between a homeless stranger's
long alabaster fingers.
For those that don't,
that hang, 108—
they dance
the steady jive of the pendulum and metronome.
A white bag of clothes
sits behind the stranger's seat as he publicly practices his faith,
in this sanctuary divorced from a singular tradition.

He is a wanderer, homeless like the
many who find refuge here,
with his matted salt and peppered tendrils,
and big delphinium eyes in love with staring blankly, more at home in the
library
than its first and true residents, the books themselves.

In the library, with its incessant conversations,
cellphones beeping and vibrating,
the mad drumming of keyboards,
and the wail of irate babies,
he muses.

The urban nomad meditates, knowing elusive calm,
in his home that is not his home, and yet it is,
just like it is also the home of many with nowhere to go,
in the not-as-quiet as it once was library.

Ode

Ochre, sienna,
white phosphorous
and obsidian children
live the song
between whips
and bullets,

live the song
of American dawn,
planted like the
morning glory,
the sycamore,
and the poplar tree

on the backs of
the spirited away,
those who hail
from the dream(ed),
mother continent
of muses, intellect,
moonless darkness, myth,
technology, and humanity,
of primordial ancestors
that would become all shades—
Africa, land eternal
of the night children
of the highest genetic diversity,
of our captured, sold off,
and enslaved ancestors
once foolishly counted
as property amongst
poultry, bovine,
and swine.

And out of that shack of history
with its chorus of heavy raindrops
on tin roofs, and branch-swept dirt floors,
there comes the true nightmare,
that true deception
of the American dream.

We know what gathers
in the promised land,
from the oldest stories
to the newest dreams,
and weep for its glory
beneath sewn eyelids.

We know what gathers in the promised land,
and in our divisiveness,
waging war between
the pachyderm and the foal,
the promised land
of Black children,
white children,
all children
of every complexion,
of trans, intersex,
and cisgender experience,
of queer, in all its iterations,
and straight, with all its iterations alike,
is trampled in our collective fury,
set ablaze and salted for good measure
so that all the narcissi
of youth and all the wisdom of age
equally goes to fruitless dust.

Seven People Dancing

Saturday night
we were out
and the drinks
were flowing
and the men
were soft caramel,
spoonfuls of wet cinnamon,
black and creamed coffee,
all swirling sweetly
on the dance floor.

This was church
for the kids,
this club,
this house of lust,
pride, friendship,
and freedom,
where the rainbow
of sepia tones
merged and
the bodies
mingled in
every combination
that the soul
longed for—

two women
one as pretty
as a doll baby,
the other as handsome

as a young preacher
come to town
to spread
a delphinium gospel

two men,
jagged, rough-edged
obsidian knights,
kissing so tenderly
like horses
nuzzling each other
in an open field

one man,
one woman,
dancing with
gyrating hips
and tight
clenched fingers,
floating on the
ecstasy of their
reveling companions,

and then there
was the lone dancer,
an exquisite moon
surrounded on all sides
by these fellow children
of midnight
and the Lord,
full of their own spirit,
wanting someone
to ask them to dance,

but, needing no one
to do so,

'cause the music
was theirs,
'cause these folks
in this club
was theirs
just as they
belonged
to each other
'cause sometimes
one worships together
and sometimes
one worships alone,

loving the God
that gave feet
to dance,
to duck walk
and dip (erroneously
named death
drop by the straights),
to two-step,
if preferred,
and mouths
to guzzle
liquor down
and talk shit,
laugh, and
kiki for the chorus
as we damn
well pleased,

and pleased
we were,
'cause we
celebrated
our journeys,
extending
our hands
out to saints and
sinners alike,
out to victims and victimizers,
out to the courageous,
and the cowardly,
with these words,
fire blasting
from our lips—

leave the world outside and be loved,
be beloved, be yourself here,
be someone else here,
but be here, alive, beautiful,
and strong,
'cause
sacred darkness
is fading,
and only God knows
what may come by the dawn
and the opening of this cathedral.

Publication Credits

"Don't Be Like Me" published in *Blacklight Magazine* of the University of Chicago

"Underemployed While Being a Black American" published in *Apeiron Review* issue 7

"Duende" published in *Apeiron Review* issue 7

Reprint of "Duende" published in *Bombay Gin literary magazine* of Naropa University Vol. 41

"White Death Cocoon" published as a flash nonfiction piece in the *Missing Slat* (December 2015)

"Black like Me" published in the *Gambler Mag, House Wins* 2015 Edition

"When I was Little" was originally "Untitled" when published in *Kaaterskill Basin Literary Journal* issue 1.2

"Tangerine" published in *Spillway Magazine* issue 24

"Burying Blackberry with Nightshade" published in *Decomp Magazine* (December 2018)

"Carrying Coffins" published in *SLAB magazine* of Slippery Rock University (April 2019)

"Two Pairs of Black Lips" published in *Euphony Journal* of the University of Chicago (April 2019)

"Mirror of a Mirror" published in *Cortland Review* (November 2019)

"The Fair" published in *Louisville Review* (November 2019)

"A Train and a Funeral" published in *Empty Mirror* (November 2019)

"Moon Shadow" published in *Empty Mirror* (November 2019)

"From Up on High" published in *Empty Mirror* (November 2019)

"Seven People Dancing" published in *Rattle* (November 2019)

"Swim Swim" published by *The Daily Drunk* (July 2020)

"Don't Call Me Middle Class" published in *Eunoia Review* (September 2020)

"Luciferous Child" forthcoming in *Rhino Poetry* (2024)

About the Author

Denzel Xavier Scott debuted as an author of genre literature in November 2021 in *Beneath Ceaseless Skies* with his short story, "The Black Rainbow." His poem, "Questions for the Coming Age of the God of Meat" was published by *Fiyah Magazine* in January of 2023 and his short story, "Zariel: Parable of a Gifted Black Child" is forthcoming in the January/February 2024 issue of *Fantasy and Science Fiction (F&SF) Magazine*. He was recently named as a Cave Canem Fellow Semifinalist for his then-unpublished and then-named debut collection, *Hymnal of a Delphinium Moon*, was a Pushcart nominee in 2020 as well as a Sundress Press Best-of-the-Net finalist in poetry in 2019 and has twice been nominated for inclusion in the Best New Poets anthology. He earned his BA in English from the University of Chicago and received his Writing MFA at the Savannah College of Art and Design (SCAD) in his hometown, Savannah, GA. His essays, literary fiction, nonfiction, and literary poetry appear in *Spillway, Rattle, Decomp, Pidgeonholes, Empty Mirror, the Cortland Review, Random Sample Review, Linden Avenue*, amongst many others.

You can find him often on Twitter in real-time at: twitter.com/DenzelScott